D1413846

# CITIES AT WAR

## PARIS

★ ★ ★

## Nathan Aaseng

New York

Maxwell Macmillan Canada
Toronto

Maxwell Macmillan International
New York  Oxford  Singapore  Sydney

PHOTOGRAPHIC ACKNOWLEDGMENTS
Front Cover: The Bettmann Archive
Back Cover: The Bettmann Archive
Interiors: AP—Wide World Photos: 4, 9, 19, 87
The Bettmann Archive: 11, 13, 14, 16, 17, 18, 20, 22, 25,
26-27, 28, 30, 33, 34-35, 37, 38, 39, 40, 42, 44, 47, 50, 52,
55, 56-57, 58, 61, 64, 69, 71, 74, 77, 80-81, 83, 84-85, 86,
88, 89, 91

Map on pages 6-7: Kathie Kelleher

New Discovery Books
Macmillan Publishing Company
866 Third Avenue
New York, NY 10022

Maxwell Macmillan Canada, Inc.
1200 Eglinton Avenue East
Suite 200
Don Mills, Ontario M3C 3N1

Macmillan Publishing Company is part of the Maxwell Communication
Group of Companies.

First Edition

Printed in the United States of America

10 9 8 7 6 5 4 3 2 1


**Library of Congress Cataloging-in-Publication Data**
Aaseng, Nathan.
    Paris / by Nathan Aaseng.
        p.   cm. — (Cities at War).
    Includes bibliographical references and index.
    Summary: Describes life in Paris, France, during World War II.
    ISBN 0-02-700010-9
    1. World War, 1939–1945—France—Paris—Juvenile literature. 2.
Paris (France)—History—1940–1944—Juvenile literature.   [1. Paris
(France)—History—1940–1944. 2. World War, 1939–1945—
France—Paris.]   I. Title. II. Series.
D802.F82P3728   1992
944' .36—dc20                                        92-709

# CONTENTS

★ ★ ★

*Dancing in the City of Light before the darkness of World War II*

# 1

# DARKNESS IN THE CITY OF LIGHT

Paris was *the* place to be in the eyes of many young people around the world in the spring of 1940. In contrast to the darkening clouds of war spreading across Europe from Nazi Germany, Paris still shone as the City of Light.

The French capital had stood out for centuries as a focal point of the highest aims of Western civilization. Paris was in the forefront of culture, fashion, and modern industry. The City of Light attracted creative souls from all over the world. Artists, authors, musicians, poets, philosophers, and directors gathered in droves to soak up the city's atmosphere of culture.

★ ★ ★

Paris was also famous for its beauty. Even the heavy industry that pumped wealth into the city was hidden behind hills where the smoke-belching factories could not mar the landscape. From its open flower markets, old neighborhoods, and sidewalk cafes, to its wide avenues and fashionable nightlife, Paris poured on the charm that was a source of pride for residents and pleasure for tourists. In 1940, a journalist was moved to write that Paris "has probably given more happiness to more people than any place that ever existed."[1]

Even the origins of Paris were steeped in romantic myth. The city was linked in some tales to Paris of Troy, who started the Trojan War by running off with the Greek beauty, Helen. Legend had it

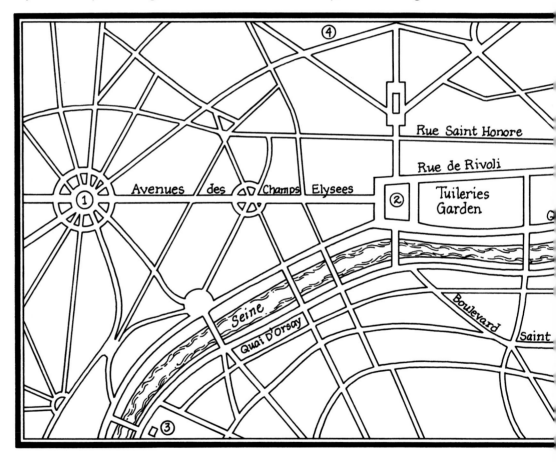

that Paris made his way to northern France and founded the city that bore his name. In reality, more than 2,000 years ago a Gallic tribe known as the Parisii settled in a valley of the Seine River. Located at an important crossroads of river and land routes, their community grew into an important city. The Roman legions who later conquered the city called it by the Latin name *Lutetia*, or "Midwater dwelling," and designated it the capital city of the region. Several centuries later, following the withdrawal of the Romans, the city was renamed Paris.

Paris's grace and beauty took shape over the centuries. Arti-

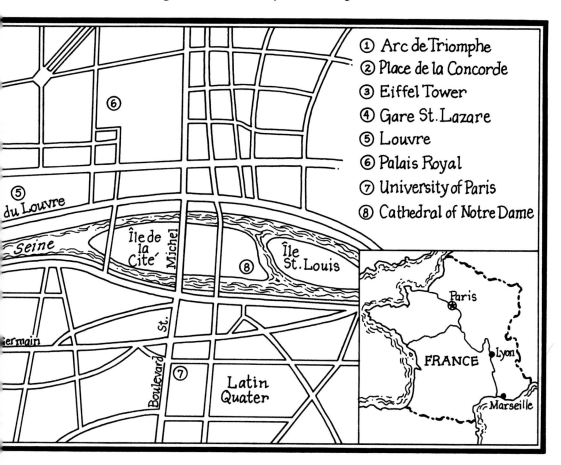

① Arc de Triomphe
② Place de la Concorde
③ Eiffel Tower
④ Gare St. Lazare
⑤ Louvre
⑥ Palais Royal
⑦ University of Paris
⑧ Cathedral of Notre Dame

sans and laborers worked on the massive cathedral of Notre Dame, begun in the 12th century, for more than a hundred years. A sprawling palace was turned into the Louvre, home of world-renowned art treasures. Paris's Left Bank (of the Seine River) became the haven for intellectuals.

Even while developing its charm, Paris saw its share of war. Viking assaults in the 9th century gave way to the Hundred Years' War with England in the 14th century. French turned upon French in the bloody Revolution of 1789.

More recently, Paris's neighbor to the east posed the greatest menace. Young people living in Paris in 1940 had heard many stories of war with Germany. Their grandparents had told of the terrible days in 1871, during the Franco-Prussian War, when the Germans captured and looted Paris. Their parents had spoken with sorrow of the horrible slaughter of nearly 1.5 million French soldiers that World War I had brought some 20 years earlier.

But in the spring of 1940, the young people of Paris had no real knowledge of war. A visitor at that time would never have suspected that Paris was a city at war with a powerful enemy.

Technically, France had been at war with Germany since that country's lightning conquest of Poland in September 1939. But there had been no real fighting yet between the French and the Nazi armies of Adolf Hitler, the chancellor of Germany. The press began to speak of *le drôle guerre*—the phony war.

Even when German forces ended the phony war with a sudden all-out attack on France's small northern neighbors in May 1940, few Parisians showed concern for their personal safety. While conscious of the threat of war, they believed their three-million-man army, equipped with the world's largest arsenal of tanks, to be the world's most effective fighting force. That army was dug in behind

*Citizens of Paris relax in a cafe on the beautiful Left Bank.*

the Maginot Line, a costly series of steel and concrete fortifications that supposedly sealed France off from invasion from the east.

According to the French media, the German army did not pose a serious threat. Gilles Perrault, a young adolescent at the time, later recalled that "for many months the French press had been making sarcastic remarks about the German army."[2] The Germans were said to be ill-equipped, undertrained, and likely to crack under the strain of battle.

The first stunning reports of German victory in Holland, Belgium, and Luxembourg pricked the nerves of some of the people of Paris. Official sources of information stayed ominously quiet.

The rumors and snatches of news that filtered through from the battlefront were disastrous. Within three weeks, France and its allies were routed. The Belgian and Dutch armies surrendered, and the British barely escaped back to England from a disastrous battle at Dunkirk, France. German troops swarmed through a breach they punched in the Maginot Line. Thousands of terrified refugees from northeastern France poured into Paris at all hours of the day and night.

Yet in June 1940, remembers one Parisian, "we remained gay and confident."[3] Young people heard again the stories of how the German forces had tried for years to drive into Paris during World War I. Although the Germans had once reached the outskirts of the city, its defenses had always held. Except for the walls of sandbags erected to protect precious buildings such as Notre Dame Cathedral from being caught in the crossfire between armies, life in Paris changed little in 1940.

The bubble of confidence shielded the French from reality. With their allies routed, their own troops soundly beaten, and Germany's powerful air force ruling the skies, France's position was

*The Paris Opera House is made ready for the possibility of German attack.*

hopeless. On June 3, German bombers flew over Paris and devastated the huge Citroen industrial plant. PARIS BOMBED! screamed huge headlines in the newspapers. Yet one reporter who toured the city afterward found citizens unconcerned about the war. They seemed unable to comprehend the idea of the French army being defeated.

In the second week of June, the Germans rolled toward Paris with nothing but the shattered remnants of the French army standing in the way. Sensing that Germany was moving in for the kill, Italy raced for its share of the spoils and declared war on France. Desperate to spare the city from ruin, the French government declared Paris an open city. That meant that no effort would be made to defend it. The proud City of Light, so secure in its own might, was surrendered to the enemy without a struggle.

News of the surrender hit Paris like a tidal wave on June 11. Stores closed immediately. The main avenues leading out of town, which only hours before had been filled with complacent, unhurried French citizens, were now so choked with panic-stricken people fleeing the approach of their ancient enemy that "you could not tell the sidewalks from the streets."[4]

"I am going to pull up stakes before night, with my parents," one young woman told news photographer Philippe Boegner. "I have no desire to be violated. Those are savages, that is what my father who was wounded in 1916 told me."[5] Parisians fled in cars and horse-drawn carts, on bicycles and wheelbarrows, and on foot, carrying as many of their hastily packed belongings as they could. For a long time only those on foot made much progress through the snarled traffic.

The population of the metropolitan area of Paris had swollen to five million, more than double its size, with the influx of refugees

from the north. Now, more than four million people tried to abandon the city at once.

Included in that number were many youngsters sent away to the safety of the countryside. For the most part, the evacuation was helter-skelter. One resident, Denise Frank, remembers, "I was 19 myself and had just started my first teaching assignment when the orders of evacuation came" from a messenger of the ministry of education. "With a group of 25 children 5 to 12 years of age, we traveled southward."[6] A reporter remembered seeing many youngsters, frightened and bewildered by the sudden change in their lives,

*A train filled with evacuated schoolchildren leaves Paris for the safety of the countryside.*

13

*Parisian parents read notices that tell them where they can contact their evacuated children.*

grumbling as they fought through the crowds, carrying or pushing their heavy loads.

German and Italian warplanes, cruising the skies without opposition, swooped down on the long columns of panic-stricken civilians on the highways leading out of Paris. Refugees heard the whistling of the bombs, and, in the words of one witness, each time "everyone thought it was for him."[7] More than 40,000 refugees are believed to have died on their flight from the city. Those who survived arrived at their destinations exhausted and famished, having had no food for days.

A number of children were separated from their parents during the two-day torrent of refugees on the southbound roads. For weeks afterward, Paris newspapers were filled with pleas from frantic parents who had lost track of their little ones, and with notices of lost children who had been found.

On Thursday, June 13, the streets that had been swimming in chaos fell silent as a tomb. The once-beautiful city was enshrouded in a thick black smoke that reeked and coated the hands and faces of those who remained. Only later did Parisians learn the cause: fires from Paris's fuel-oil depots were set ablaze by the French army to prevent them from falling into German hands. The odor, the soot, and the darkness reinforced the sense of doom that hung over the city. No one knew where the Germans were, when they would arrive, or what they would do when they came. Few people opened their windows or ventured into the streets.

The first German infantry troops entered the City of Light at dawn on June 14 and were greeted by silence and emptiness. The Nazis later showed a newsreel of throngs of Parisians cheering the regiments of German soldiers that goose-stepped down the Champs Elysées, the city's most famous avenue. This led many to believe that the people of Paris welcomed the arrival of the Germans. But that film was actually of a parade staged several days later, when the streets were lined with Germans who had arrived to administer the captured city.

There were, in fact, some French men and women who, discontented with their own inept government, were pleased that the Germans had come. Others were so terrified by the awesome spec-

*The German army rolls into Paris.*

tacle of heavily armed, highly disciplined Nazi troops that they would do almost anything to please their conquerors. Some cafe owners offered free drinks to the soldiers. According to one report, "a girl ran out to present a small bunch of flowers to a German officer. With measured contempt, he threw them to the sidewalk and ground them under the heel of his boot."[8]

But most French were stunned and sickened by the sight of

*French citizens sell souvenirs to Nazi soldiers as they ride through the Place de la Concorde.*

*Triumphant German forces parade under the majestic Arc de Triomphe.*

foreign troops marching around their cherished monuments. Young people especially felt betrayed by their leaders, by the entire political system that had produced too much squabbling among rival parties to function effectively, by their army, and by the press that had duped them with lies of French invincibility and German bungling. Almost overnight, their world had changed. Their security had been stripped. There had been no battle. Most Parisians had seen no bombing, no violence, none of the wholesale destruction that typically visited the city of a defeated army, but only sudden and shameful defeat.

"The terrible thing has happened,"[9] the citizens of Paris whispered in disbelief. Many who cautiously ventured out into the

*A proud Frenchman weeps as he watches his beloved city taken over by the Germans.*

*Soon after the Germans entered Paris, the hated Nazi swastika began appearing over public buildings.*

city later that morning cried openly when huge flags bearing the Iron Cross and the swastika, symbols of the Nazi government, were raised on France's sacred Arc de Triomphe in midmorning of June 14. More than a dozen Parisians committed suicide. The only hints of resistance were a single French soldier who opened fire on the advancing Germans before being gunned down, and the sabotaging of the Eiffel Tower elevator to deny the enemy the satisfaction of looking down over the conquered city.

France officially surrendered to Germany three days later. According to the terms of the treaty, the southwestern portion of France was allowed to remain free. Its government, however, based at the town of Vichy, agreed to abide by Nazi wishes. The northeastern section, including Paris, was now under the enemy's control, which extended itself throughout most of Europe. Germany's military might had grown so powerful that it was difficult even for the young to envision a day when they would again be free in the City of Light.

*Acting more like tourists than a conquering army, German soldiers take pictures of the Eiffel Tower.*

# 2

## GERMANY'S PRIZE

"War," a grim United States Civil War general, William T. Sherman, once said, "is hell." The older people of Paris knew well the truth of that statement. They had seen muddy trenches strewn with the dead bodies of hundreds of thousands of their sons and brothers and husbands during World War I, and that was a war they had won.

This time they had lost, and the shock was so great that they did not know how to react. The typically outgoing Parisians "instinctively withdrew into the family circle for warmth and protection."[1]   And yet circumstances were nowhere near as brutal or horrifying as they had expected. Paris was spared the savage punishment that the Nazis had inflicted upon Warsaw, the captured capital of Poland.

The City of Light owed its salvation to its dazzling reputation, which had claimed the admiration of even France's archenemy, Adolf Hitler. Paris was Hitler's prize conquest. He wanted Paris to be preserved as a holiday wonderland, a bustling city of enchantments where battle-weary German soldiers could be sent for a week of entertainment and relaxation as a reward for their services.

Germany's occupying troops were ordered to be polite, respectful, even helpful. In many ways, they seemed nothing more than a large group of tourists, carrying their cameras everywhere, visiting the attractions. Reporter Philippe Boegner reported that it was "impossible to discern on their faces any satisfaction from their victory."[2] He described a scene in which a German soldier tried very hard to make friends with some youngsters playing in the street. The soldier smiled and showed them his watch, his camera, and a pen to let them know that Germans were not monsters.

The occupiers of Paris played on the young people's feeling of betrayal. Posters were put up throughout the city, showing a handsome, smiling German soldier feeding a French child while other French children look on in admiration. The caption read, "You have been abandoned. Put your trust in the German soldier."[3]

German soldiers were also considerate of the city's treasures. For example, they never failed to fuel the eternal flame that burned at the Tomb of the Unknown Soldier under the Arc de Triomphe.

The Germans encouraged the French to resume their lives just as they had been before the occupation. Public services such as banks, shops, and transportation systems were back in operation within days of the German arrival. Paris's own police were back walking their beats on the street. On July 18, just a month after the German arrival, 700 schools were in full session in the city. By October, many of the refugees who had fled in terror had trickled back to find almost all institutions, from prisons to hospitals to churches,

*Pedestrians stop to look at a German bookstore, which opened shortly after the Nazi invasion.*

*German guards
keep watch
outside a hotel.*

*One of the many cafes in Paris reserved for Germans only*

operating very much as they always had. So intent were the Germans on maintaining the good life in Paris that the city operated on a far more normal schedule during the war than did any place in Germany.

Parisians reacted to this relatively mild treatment in a variety of ways. Once over the initial agony of defeat, many of the citizens felt relief that they had been spared the usual horrors of war. Reporters spoke of a "euphoria" among the French that no great calamity had accompanied their defeat.

Some welcomed the Nazis as their salvation from the Communists who had been actively pursuing power in Paris. Right-wing anti-Jewish groups also admired the German government. The Nazis tapped into these feelings to recruit more than 100,000 French to fight in German uniform during the course of the war, many of them joining the German offensive against the communist Soviet Union.

Others, awed by the power and precision of the goose-stepping German military ranks, were scared of offending the conquerors. They hoped that if they treated the invaders well and did whatever they asked, they would receive lenient treatment. Some of them even engaged the German soldiers in good-natured teasing about their situation, as if the French were good sports who had lost a friendly card game, not a war.

Other Parisians, with a deeper pride in their heritage, were so shamed by their defeat that they sought scapegoats and alibis to account for their woeful showing against German forces. Communists, the press, army generals, and Jews were among those blamed for the defeat.

The majority of both young and old resigned themselves to making the best of their new situation, which they admitted was not

*After the invasion, Parisian newsstands were forced to sell German papers and magazines.*

likely to improve in the near future. Life under the Germans was not so terrible that it could not be tolerated. Outwardly the Parisians showed neither fear nor hope. They were not meek, timid, or submissive, only indifferent, as if the German presence was no more of a nuisance than a heat wave. The mood of the city was curiously detached, and it led more than one observer to comment in amazement, "I haven't seen the symptoms of real hatred in any-one."[4]

As a result, hundreds of German soldiers and French citizens mingled in the streets every day without any problems. Many French students abandoned the study of English as a second language and turned to German. The merchants of Paris found that the Germans were willing to do business with them. Some of them found that they could live quite prosperously if they managed to work themselves into the good graces of the German authorities. French factories poured out many of the war materials that fed the German army. Hotels were filled to capacity as more than 500 of them were requisitioned by the Germans to house government officials and soldiers. Expensive restaurants drew a steady stream of German customers. More than 100 nightclubs advertised in German for German customers. For the first six months of the occupation, Paris seemed peacefully resigned to its fate as Germany's prize jewel.

Many younger Parisians were ashamed at how easily some of their elders accepted their new masters. Where were the heroes in a city that had surrendered without a fight, a city in which so many people willingly did exactly as their conquerors asked? Why were the Nazis being treated so politely, as if they were guests instead of invaders? Where was the sense of outrage, defiance, patriotism?

"I am renouncing my country, I no longer want to be

French," wrote Micheline Bood, a teenager at the time. "When you see how one and all are licking the boots of the Germans out of fear and cowardice, even in my own family! I am terribly sickened by this lousy country."[5]

Despite the intense German efforts to maintain business as usual, the people of Paris found their lives changed in countless ways. But even those who hated the Germans admitted that not every change was for the worse. The streets of Paris, which had formerly been bustling with hundreds of thousands of automobiles, were quieter and the air much cleaner than any of the young people had ever known. "Paris had never looked more beautiful," said Gilles Perrault. "The air was as pure as country air."[6]

But even this small pleasure served as a reminder of something far more valuable that the French had lost—freedom. Automobiles and the gasoline to power them were privileges given only to the occupiers and to a few select French. In November 1940, only 7,000 automobiles were licensed in Paris, mostly to doctors, hospitals, the press (which was subject to German censors), and high-ranking government officials. As gasoline became increasingly scarce, many of these cars had to be fitted with a special device to run on natural gas. The residents of Paris reverted to more basic forms of transportation—walking and biking. More than two million bicycles would be cruising the streets before the end of the war. These were converted to all kinds of uses, such as hauling freight, pulling trailers, and carrying infants. Even taxi services converted to *vélotaxis*—flimsy, custom-designed, two-passenger carriages pulled by bicycles. Tandem bicycles and horse-drawn cabs were also used. In this automobile-free environment, the youth of Paris, with their strong young legs and energy, became the speed kings and queens of the streets.

*Bicycle taxis bring a bride and groom to their wedding after gasoline rationing reduced the number of cars in the city.*

*During the war years, bicycles became a familiar sight on Paris's streets.*

The only alternative to walking and biking was mass transit. Paris's subway system, the metro, was overwhelmed by the sudden demand. Trains were crammed at all hours of the day.

The people of Paris could hardly move without seeing or hearing the marks of their German conquerors. Huge swastikas hung from many buildings and monuments. The French tricolor flag was banned from public places. Intersections were cluttered with posts stacked with black-and-white signs that gave directions and street names in German. Conductors on the trains called out the stops in German as well as French.

Many Parisians later remembered a particularly humiliating German rite, a "daily slap in the face":[7] Every morning the Germans would parade down to the Arc de Triomphe in full uniform, with their bands playing and flags flying.

The city's police force was yet another reminder of Paris's defeat. Although Parisians, they took their orders without question from the German authorities. In normal times, the policemen on the streets paid no particular heed to army personnel. But now, Parisians watched their own police salute the German officers who rode by in their Mercedes staff cars.

Even music was not immune from the stamp of the German occupiers. The audiences that attended concerts, now organized by the Germans, noticed a glaring change in the programs. German waltzes were played first, before any of the music of French composers.

Even the clocks of Paris served as constant reminders of the city's masters. The Germans insisted that Paris clocks be set to Berlin time, which was two hours earlier than Paris. They also imposed a curfew on Paris, which was set at various hours depending on the mood of the authorities. This disrupted some traditions, par-

*German soldiers tour one of the historic districts of Paris.*

*A day in the country: Nazi troops prepare for a sightseeing trip around Paris.*

ticularly religious services at Christmastime. In heavily Roman Catholic Paris, the Christmas evening mass, usually held at midnight, had to be moved back to 5:40 P.M. in order to get everyone home on time.

The students of Paris found empty classrooms and open

desks when they returned to their schools. Thousands of their class-mates were gone, evacuated before the city fell into enemy hands. Those who remained discovered that their textbooks had been altered. Pages from history books were missing or pasted together, the work of the German censors. One student later remembered his

*With the help of a French gendarme, a German soldier checks the identification of people entering a Nazi-occupied building.*

*Parisians on line for a movie, the most popular form of entertainment during the war years.*

principal reading a message to the class from French president Philippe Pétain. A World War I hero, the 84-year-old president now advocated cooperation with the Germans.

The authorities encouraged entertainment as a tool for keeping the people from dwelling on their loss of liberty, and they found plenty of takers. Box-office receipts at the cinema during the height of World War II were triple those of prewar times.

But as much as the occupation government tried to keep spirits light in the city, the effort was doomed from the start. There was no way to sugarcoat the fact that Germany was the enemy of France, an enemy who felt free to plunder the country's riches. Despite relentless propaganda to convince people otherwise, this enemy's policies would prove to be cruel beyond imagination. Every day that Paris remained a prisoner, its citizens grew more resentful of the Nazi overlords. Under such conditions, the honeymoon between Paris and its occupiers could not last long.

*A swastika indicates that a restaurant is for German soldiers only.*

# 3

# THE OPPRESSION MOUNTS

Many Parisian merchants, government officials, police, and young people continued to do the bidding of their German masters throughout the war, either out of greed or out of fear for their own survival. One Parisian spoke with contempt of "boys and girls laughing and cuddling in cinemas. Nothing is going on as far as they are concerned."[1] Many teenage girls went out on dates and became romantically involved with German soldiers.

But while the German soldiers usually behaved properly, even gallantly, around women and small children, they could react brutally against those who did not show what they thought was proper respect. A teenage boy who did not jump out of the way of a German soldier could expect a brutal kick to remind him that the

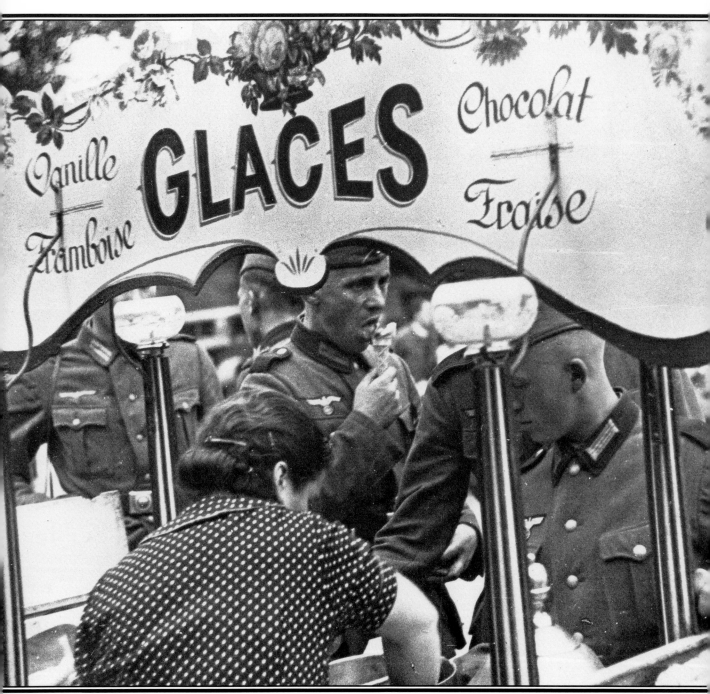

*The Germans claimed many French goods, including ice cream, for their own use.*

French were defeated people. Any sign of resentment from the citizens of Paris was dealt with harshly, and young people could be arrested for the most minor offenses. One boy was caught spitting at a photograph of a German movie star at the cinema and was hauled off to jail.

On the night of November 10, 1941, a young man named Jacques Bonsergent got mixed up in a scuffle between German soldiers and some French youths. Bonsergent was the only one caught, and even though he had only been trying to break up the fight, he was executed for striking a German soldier. He was the first of thousands of Parisians executed by the German authorities.

The German authorities took great advantage of the French to line their pockets. France was forced to pay the equivalent of millions of dollars per day to Germany to "compensate" it for the cost of the war.

Although the Germans paid the merchants for their wares and services, they greatly inflated the value of German currency. As a result, Germans went on a spending spree and made off with most of the consumer goods in Paris for a fraction of their real cost. French merchants were stuck with the loss, and little quality merchandise was left for the people of Paris. In addition, thousands of priceless paintings and other works of art were removed from Parisian art galleries and carted off to Germany. "They are taking everything we have," the people muttered.[2]

When the results of a campaign to entice the French into working for the German war industries failed to satisfy the authorities, harsher methods were imposed. Despite its claims of benevolence, Germany held nearly two million French prisoners of war and used them as hostages, promising families the release of one prisoner for every three French workers who volunteered to work in the factories of Germany.

This, too, failed to produce the desired results. The police were then dispatched to round up workers for the German war effort. Although many personnel files had been removed or destroyed by the French government before the arrival of the Germans, the authorities used a system of work permits and ration cards to keep tabs on the people. They patrolled cinema exits and the métro and infiltrated crowds in working-class districts. Anyone they caught without a proper work permit could be arrested and sent to a German factory. The authorities also located likely candidates for work and pulled them out of their houses. Many parents without permits had to move around the city constantly with their families to avoid being tracked down and sent off to German factories. Many were not successful. More than a million French, a substantial number of them from Paris, were sent to work in Germany during the war.

By far the worst treatment was reserved for the Jews, whom the Nazis blamed for most of the ills of society. Many Jews from eastern Europe had fled to Paris to escape persecution at the hands of the Nazis. There would be no escape this time. The Germans had scarcely entered the city when harassment of Jews began, much of it from the right-wing French. Jews had already been singled out as scapegoats for France's humiliation. German censors controlled all aspects of publishing and information—and the vicious propaganda of the anti-Jewish French created a general atmosphere of intolerance.

The persecution began with humiliation. Jews were attacked and ridiculed by the press and government officials. On September 27, 1940, German authorities required Jewish business operators to post notices at their places of business that they were Jewish. More restrictive laws were passed. Jews were banned from most public

*The persecution of Jews begins: The doors of a popular Paris cafe read "Only for Aryans."*

places, including movie theaters, phone booths, and even the lines that commonly formed in front of food shops as food became scarce.

Before long a more sinister Nazi policy was put into effect as Hitler's government decided that its "final solution" in dealing with the Jews of Europe was to annihilate them. In May 1941, more than 6,000 Jews were rounded up and sent to different centers in Paris. In August of that year, another 6,000 Jewish men, women, and children were dragged from their homes for "processing." On March 27, 1942, the first trains rolled out of Paris. Unknown to the deportees, they were headed for the concentration camp at Auschwitz in Poland. Immediately upon arriving, many of these Jews were sent to the gas chambers.

Later that spring, the authorities decreed that all Jews in German-occupied territories aged six and up must wear yellow stars on their clothing. This enabled the Germans to mark their victims for the death that awaited them. A Jewish youth who dashed out the door to school without putting on his or her yellow-starred jacket could be arrested and shipped off in the sinister trains.

July 17, 1942, was the darkest of all days in the former City of Light. A massive campaign that day herded together for deportation more than 13,000 non-French Jews living in Paris. They were given only a couple of hours' notice, and few of them suspected their fate. Included in the roundup were more than 3,000 children, from infants to 12 year olds, who were dumped in a small stadium built for bicycle racing. From there, many were transferred to a four-story concrete compound in the town of Drancy, three miles northeast of Paris.

Gina Rosenblum, the Paris-born daughter of Polish immigrants, was ten years old when her family was taken to the bicycle stadium: "There we were escorted into buses, along with thousands of children who were crying, and old people, some being dragged in pitiful states of health. People screamed all night long. Women threw themselves off the top of stands. I can still hear the screams."

She and her five-year-old sister were separated from their parents and moved to Drancy, "where we lived for some weeks in terrible conditions. I don't want to relate the horror of it."[3]

Many Jewish children spent weeks in filthy, crowded captivity, with virtually no food, overrun with lice and disease. Small children, torn from their parents, cried and screamed all night long in their terror and loneliness. They were searched and robbed of their few belongings. The heart-wrenching despair is captured in the last letter of a 7-year-old girl, written to her landlady and delivered by a Red Cross worker. "I am writing to you because I have nobody else. Last week Papa was deported. Mama has been deported, too. I have lost my purse. I have nothing left."[4]

Then the trains arrived. Older children climbed aboard first to help the younger ones onto these death wagons. The trains continued to roll until more than 12,000 Jews of Paris were sent off to concentration camps. Of the 13,000 arrested in July, only 30 survived deportation to Auschwitz. Even when the German war machine was collapsing, the Nazis diverted crucial resources to feed their malice toward Jews. In July 1944, a group of Jewish schoolchildren was deported to the death camps along with their teacher.

Some of the Paris police were sickened by their role in all this, but for the most part, they made the arrests without protest. In fact, the French government showed so much enthusiasm for handing its own citizens over to the Nazis that even the German officers felt contempt for it. Although a number of Parisian Christians sewed

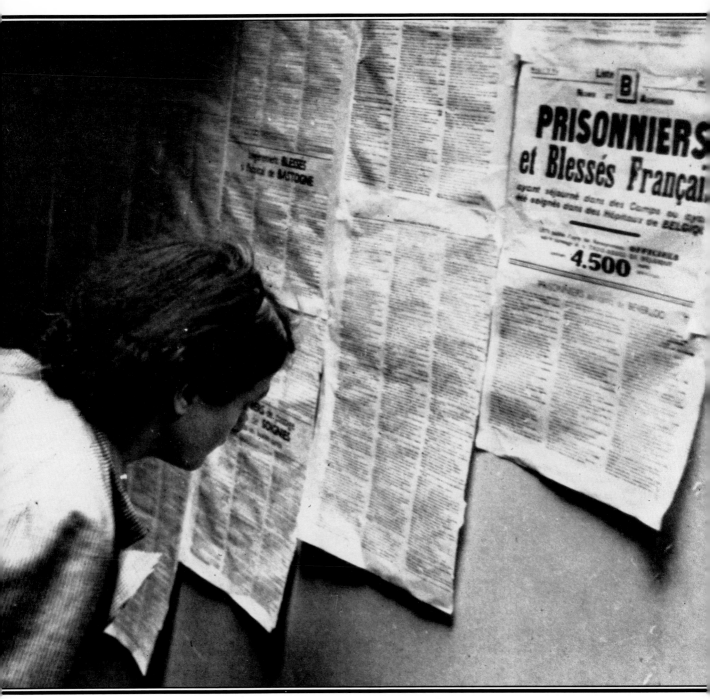

*A woman scans the lists of people imprisoned by the Germans for the name of her missing husband.*

yellow stars onto their clothing in protest, and some helped hide Jews, most Parisians paid little attention to the plight of the Jews.

The people of Paris were caught up in their own injustices which, while mild compared to the fates of their Jewish neighbors, were nonetheless severe. They watched bitterly as those unscrupulous people who learned to make themselves useful to the occupiers prospered as never before. Some of these despised collaborators paraded around with their fancy clothes and expensive belongings, ate in the most elegant restaurants, drank the most expensive champagne, spent their leisure time at the horse races, and accumulated fortunes.

At the same time, the children saw the anguish of their hardworking, honest parents who were forced to cheat, smuggle, steal, and beg in order to keep their families alive. "It was no small hardship having to throw our moral scruples to the winds," wrote one parent, "and settle down to a dishonest way of life in full view of the children, and in contradiction to all we were striving to teach them."[5]

The people of Paris were steadily being ground down into the dust of poverty. This poverty became so widespread and severe that it would dominate the memories of the young people of Paris during the occupation.

*Once rationing began, Parisians spent hours standing in line for food and other goods.*

# 4

# MISERY

While still wobbly from the shock of occupation, Paris was brought to its knees by a cruel twist of nature in the late autumn of 1940. Winter arrived early and struck hard. The winter of 1940-1941 proved to be the longest, coldest, snowiest winter that the people of Paris had ever known.

Most families in Paris were left without any defense against this arctic onslaught. With industry and transportation disrupted and fuel supplies diverted to Germany's war needs, Parisians had almost no access to energy sources. Heating oil was unavailable, and shipments of coal to the city were few and far between. The coal that was rationed out by the German authorities could not begin to warm a house. The typical monthly supply doled out by the government was barely enough to heat a one-room apartment for five days. To conserve energy, classrooms were open only half a day during the winter.

"Family life went on in one or two rooms only," remembers Gilles Perrault.[1] He recalls wearing many layers of clothing while reading books, and fumbling to turn the pages with mittened hands.

Those who lived through the occupation remembered later that they were always cold in Paris during the winters all through the war. "Men and women, but especially children, blew fiercely on their hands in an effort to warm them. Their fingers were red and swollen. . . gaped with cracks or oozed pus from running sores."[2]

The people of Paris retreated into the underground passages of the metro and into public buildings such as post offices. They crowded onto sidewalk grilles to feel the warm air that escaped from the subway, and stuffed newspaper into their clothing as extra insulation.

Weekends were the worst because few warm public buildings were open. "Get the Saturday or Sunday meal over and done with and the household chores finished, and go to bed with a hot-water bottle for your feet," advised one Parisian.[3]

The cold pushed people to the limits of their endurance. One woman swallowed her pride and requested that German officers be stationed in her suburban home. German soldiers were assured of adequate comfort. With them under her roof, the woman would be allotted an extra supply of coal to keep the house warm, so her small children would not suffer.

Electricity was in equally short supply. Families crowded under a single light bulb to accomplish their tasks after sundown. Movie theaters fashioned their own bicycle-powered generators to keep their projectors operating.

Inflation robbed the French of what little earning power they had. Many Parisians, realizing that their money was rapidly becom-

*An open air market offers very little during the cruel winter of 1940-1941.*

*French women
wait on line for
food in front of a
store displaying
empty tins in its
windows.*

*A vendor stands with an empty cart in what was once a thriving farmers market.*

ing worthless, spent it as quickly as they could. By the end of the war, prices had soared so high that a bicycle cost as much as the prewar price of an automobile.

Soap disappeared from the store shelves. Few medicines could be purchased. Many Parisians were forced to walk everywhere, but when their shoes wore out, there was no leather to either make new shoes or repair the old ones. Many people resorted to wooden shoes.

The worst hardship borne by the people of Paris during the occupation was hunger. Without the basic nourishment to live, nothing else in life had importance. As food supplies became scarce, the Parisians became more and more obsessed with the problem of finding their next scrap of food.

Food shortages were anticipated early by the occupiers, who introduced a rationing program in September 1940, only months after entering the city. Parisians formed lines on school playgrounds to receive their ration cards, which were issued according to age. Children under 3 were classified as Es, ages 3-6 were J1s, ages 6-13 were J2s, and ages 13-21 were J3s. All food, except artichokes, cabbages, and rutabagas, was rationed, and the amount of the ration varied according to a person's classification.

But rationing hardly solved the shortages. Denise Frank relates, "My parents had a difficult job providing food, as everything was with tickets, in very small amounts, and you had to wait in line for hours. The bread was very dark, mixed with straw."[4] Women slept on porches near the food stores so that they could be near the front of the line when the stores opened.

In many cases, the rations could do little more than whet the appetite for a real meal. A typical ration in the early days of occupation was about 12 ounces (340 grams) of bread per day, 12 ounces

(340 grams) of meat per week, and about 5 ounces (142 grams) of cheese per month. By the end of the war, even this meager allowance would have looked like a feast.

Many foods were available only to the Germans and their collaborators. In the words of one Parisian, "We have forgotten what such things as rice, butter, soap, coffee, and eggs are like."[5] Micheline Bood's diary during the winter of 1941 illustrates the dreary, restricted menu available to young people even during the milder period of food shortage:

| | |
|---|---|
| Tuesday. | Midday: beans, 2 eggs, vanilla |
| | Evening: pancakes, an egg for Papa, jam |
| Wednesday. | Midday: an egg each, vermicelli, jam |
| | Evening: beans, bean soup, jam[6] |

Watery soup was about all that the average person could afford to buy at a restaurant or cafe. Yet at the same time, high-ranking Germans and their French collaborators would be dining in the most elegant restaurants, eating whatever they wanted.

The government did subsidize basic three-course meals that people could purchase for just a few francs. At its peak, this program distributed more than a quarter of a million meals in Paris each day. But even with rationing and subsidized meals, the Parisians suffered from woefully inadequate diets. Most families in the city depended upon relatives living on farms to secretly send some of their food supplies. Those who had no relatives in the country tried to get around the authorities by privately purchasing food from farmers, an outlawed practice known as the black market.

Desperation forced families to rely on their wits for survival. Some of them tore up their lawns to plant gardens. Others kept rab-

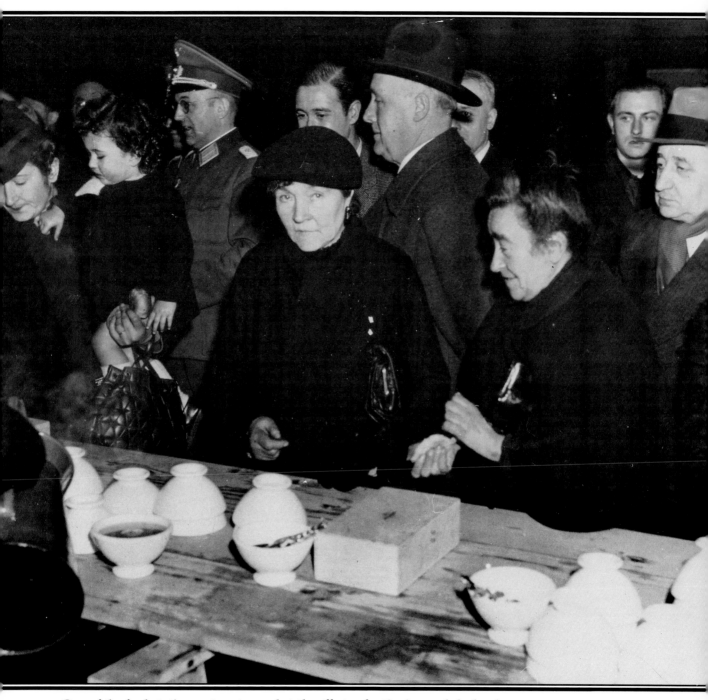

*One of the food stations set up to combat the effects of rationing and the hard winter.*

bits in their bathtubs. Boys would sneak out of their houses in the darkness of early morning to go to public parks and clip grass to bring back as rabbit food. Micheline Bood remembers stealing a pot of jam and hiding it in the school library. There she could secretly snitch fingersful during the school day.

According to Gilles Perrault, "Food haunted the imagination from morning til night. And then at night we dreamed about it."[7]

The more desperate the Parisians became, the more likely they were to resort to acts that might otherwise disgust them. Hardly a day went by without fights in the lines outside food shops. One journalist reported the disquieting news that all the cats seemed to have disappeared from Paris. It was no secret where they had gone. Cats were so commonly killed for food that farmers had to sell rabbit meat with a hind foot still attached to prove to their customers that it was not a cat.

The pitiful diet took its toll on the younger generation. According to Red Cross figures, the average child in Paris during the war ate about half the calories necessary for normal growth. Thin, frail arms and legs and bad teeth were the trademark of a generation. The average height of boys in Paris declined by nearly three inches from 1936 to 1944. Girls were, on the average, just over four inches shorter.

The Red Cross also reported more than 25,000 undernourished babies in the city. Diseases from protein and vitamin deficiency were common, especially rickets, which affects bone growth, and pellagra, a wide-ranging condition that affects the skin and the digestive and nervous systems. Deaths among infants soared, as did deaths among older children from hunger-related diseases such as tuberculosis.

Even in the worst of times, the people of Paris struggled hard to preserve the graceful traditions of their city. "Life in all of France is hard and ugly," reported *Time* magazine. "But Paris still has its old genius for softening the hardness and hiding the ugliness."[8] Although they could not afford new clothes, Parisians kept as fashionable as possible in simple, remade suits and dresses. Cookbooks were printed with recipes for making edible meals out of the meager ingredients available— for instance, a recipe for a dish made of beaten egg whites and bread crumbs dipped in milk. Many of the older citizens retained impeccable manners, even around the enemy. Children continued to play in the streets until the early curfew forced them indoors.

Yet despite their best attempts to cope with the situation, many Parisians were overwhelmed by the hardships. Gilles Perrault summed up the feelings of many children growing up during the occupation by saying, "There was no escape from the sadness except in the imagination."[9]

*Members of the French underground Resistance take a stand from an upstairs window.*

# 5

## PARIS FIGHTS BACK

T he longer the Nazis stayed, the more obvious it became that, despite their manners and propaganda, they were cruel and terrifying masters. But what could the people of Paris do against such a powerful conqueror?

There were still many who, like President Pétain, honestly believed that cooperation with the Germans was the only sane policy. Any attempt at resistance would be crushed and would provoke the vengeance of the Nazi authorities.

But as hardship, humiliation, and anger mounted over the months of the occupation, the docile reception that Paris had given its conquerors in the first months began to give way. Even those who saw no hope of overcoming the Germans' might found ways to express their feelings. The people of Paris, even the very young and old, found that one safe way of expressing what they thought of the invaders was to simply ignore them. They expressed no feelings or opinions, engaged in no conversations, and walked past the Germans as if they were not there. This silent form of protest irritated the occupation soldiers so much that they spoke of Paris as "the city that never looks at you."[1]

Another subtle form of protest among the young adults was a social misfit movement that came to be called *zazou*. Boys who were zazou wore long, oversized jackets, unpolished shoes, and wool ties and put oil in their hair. A zazou girl wore her hair long, and her wardrobe consisted mainly of short, pleated skirts, loose jackets, and flat, heavy shoes. Both sexes were partial to dark glasses and umbrellas, and they often met in cellars to dance to swing music. Many of the average citizens of Paris were shocked and disgusted by this group of idle society dropouts. But one who was involved in the zazou fashion called it "a way of showing the occupiers what we thought of them,"[2] a rebellion against the precise, orderly discipline that characterized the Germans.

Not all of the protest was silent mockery. Parisians would comfort one another by privately whispering "Paris will always be Paris."[3] Once the shock of the German military parades wore off, the French turned to private ridicule. As the daily procession of soldiers strutted down the Champs Elysées, residents would snicker, "There goes the circus."[4] They referred to the Germans as the *boches*, an ethnic slur often used to speak of Germans during World War I. Some people considered it their patriotic duty to shun the usual markets and engage in the illegal black-market trade whenever possible.

Within months of the occupation, Parisian movie-goers were hooting and heckling the German-produced newsreels shown between feature films. The authorities tried to intimidate the audiences into silence by seating policemen in the theaters, but in the darkness it was impossible to identify the culprits. Audiences became so worked up in their abuse that eventually the Germans kept the lights on in the theaters during the newsreels to discourage the audiences from getting too bold.

The first attempt at active resistance came from students. On November 11, 1940, the anniversary of France's victory over Germany in World War I, thousands of high-school and college students defied the authorities' ban on public assembly. They walked down the same avenue that the Germans paraded over every day, hands on one another's shoulders, waving flags and singing the French national anthem. "Long live France! Down with Pétain! Down with Hitler!" the students chanted.[5]

The German occupiers, who had made such an effort to be friendly and polite, sent a warning that politeness was only for those who played along: German soldiers and French police fired weapons into the air and at the feet of the demonstrators and scattered the crowd with clubs and rifle butts. One hundred twenty-three were arrested, 90 of them high-school students and 14 from college. Only a handful were convicted and sent to prison. It was a mild response by Nazi standards, but the message was clear: No form of protest would be tolerated. As an extra note of warning, the authorities executed a Parisian who had been arrested for a minor offense.

Parisian protesters walked cautiously for a while after that. Young people crept out in the dead of night to scrawl *V*s (England's symbol for victory) on building walls. In the early summer of 1941, the most daring acts of defiance were wearing black ribbons or ties on June 14 (the anniversary of Paris's fall) and wearing the French national colors of red, white, and blue on Bastille Day, France's national holiday commemorating the storming of the Bastille prison during the French Revolution of 1789. Even such timid protests prompted thousands of arrests.

True resistance did not begin in Paris until the late summer of 1941. Only two months earlier, on June 22, Germany had suddenly launched an all-out attack on the Soviet Union, the cradle of world communism. That action earned the Germans the fanatical hatred of the French Communist party. On August 21, a young Communist named Pierre Georges Fabien stalked a German officer at a metro station and shot him in the back. The officer died. The Germans responded by hanging seven members of the Communist party. Rather than squelching the resistance, the harsh measures only infuriated the Communists. They struck again and again, killing more German officers and destroying more property. The furious German authorities rounded up a pool of French hostages, many of whom were executed after each attack.

Dangerous as it was, the Resistance movement attracted many courageous young people. Since the outlawed Communists of Paris had been the first to openly fight against the German conquerors, many of the most militant youths were drawn to the party. Some of them would kill for the cause of freedom. Many more of them would die for it.

André Kirschen was a 15-year-old high-school student who joined the Resistance early. On September 10, 1941, he borrowed a handgun, walked up to a German officer standing at a ticket window, and shot him in the back.

Determined to show the futility of resistance, which had accelerated to more than 220 separate attacks during December 1941 alone, the occupying authorities brought 27 young people to a

*The Resistance on patrol in the streets of Paris*

highly publicized trial in the spring of 1942. The defendants, who had all been turned over to the German authorities by the French police, were accused of dozens of assassinations and acts of sabotage. Among them was André Kirschen.

All the defendants were found guilty by the German military court. One young woman was sent to the guillotine. Twenty-three young men were killed by firing squad. Kirschen was spared the death sentence only because he was under 16 and by military tribunal law could not be executed. While Kirschen was in prison, however, his father and brother were arrested and executed by the Gestapo (Nazi secret police).

Despite the German crackdown, the cycle of violence grew even larger. Assassins continued to strike; Germans continued to execute dozens of hostages for each incident and to torture Resistance fighters whom they caught. Nothing the authorities tried could quiet the small but determined Resistance. Although more than 1,800 French were executed in retaliation for crimes against the occupiers, the bombings and ambushes continued. Altogether, more than 500 Germans and French collaborators were assassinated.

Few of the people of Paris relished the idea of armed resistance; fewer yet approved of assassination. Most of them had been content to wait for someone to liberate them with no great cost to themselves. But the cold-blooded terrorism and the vicious reprisals of the Nazis shocked them out of their complacency. Whether Parisians liked it or not, the polite veneer that had shielded their city from the cruelties of the world war that raged around them was gone. Paris was now at war. Now, along with cold and hunger, the people of Paris came to know danger and death.

They saw it in the black-rimmed, red-ink death notices posted throughout the city. These were meant to cow the French people

**EKANNTMACHUNG** **AVIS**

Am Morgen des 21. August ist in
ris ein deutscher Wehrmachtange-
iger einem Mordanschlag zum Opfer
allen. Ich bestimme daher :

1. Sämtliche von deutschen Dienst-
llen oder für deutsche Dienststellen
Frankreich in Haft irgend einer Art
altenen Franzosen gelten vom
August ab als Geiseln.

2. Von diesen Geiseln wird bei jedem
teren Anlass eine der Schwere der
aftat entsprechende Anzahl er-
ossen werden.

Paris, den 22. August 1941.

Der Militärbefehlshaber in Frankreich
In Vertretung :
SCHAUMBURG
Generalleutnant

Le 21 août au matin, un membre
l'Armée Allemande a été victime d'u
assassinat à Paris.

En conséquence j'ordonne :

1. A partir du 23 août, tous les França
mis en état d'arrestation, quel que
soit par les autorités allemandes
France, ou qui sont arrêtés pou
celles-ci sont considérés comme otages.

2. En cas d'un nouvel acte, un nomb
d'otages correspondant à la gravité
l'acte criminel commis sera fusillé.

Paris, le 22 Août 1941.

Pour le
Militärbefehlshaber in Frankrei
SCHAUMBURG
Generalleutnant.

into giving up the struggle. But according to Gilles Perrault, they
did just the opposite. The notices were put up on a pillar near his
school. "We would go through the list of names at school; it did
not matter to us whether the dead were Jews, Communists or loy-

*A poster warns
that French
hostages will be
shot for every
German killed by
the Resistance.*

alists. They were men who had said, 'no!' " [6]

As the violence escalated, the more sinister forces within the Nazi government spread forth their lethal tentacles. The Gestapo stepped up its reign of terror. Citizens could be arrested at random and, if found to have a weapon, they were tortured or shipped off on a train, never to be seen again. Thousands of French Nazi sympathizers, many of them nothing more than sadistic bullies, were recruited for a militia whose primary purpose was to intimidate the French people.

The Resistance movement never became as powerful in Paris as it did in the rest of France. Some blamed the complacency of the Parisians, who seemed content to sit and wait for Germany to lose the war. But in fact, Paris was a suicidal place from which to wage war on the Nazis. The city was the center of all German government activity in France, as well as the center of French pro-Nazi activity. The methods of the Gestapo worked far better in the big city than in smaller towns, where everyone knew everyone else. Informers and Nazi infiltrators combed the city, sniffing out any signs of discontent, ready to make use of the Gestapo's torture rooms.

Many who had grown up talkative and trusting of their fellow Parisians found out too late how crucial it was to maintain absolute secrecy. People in the streets of the city became tight-lipped and grim, never knowing who might be listening to them. They kept to themselves or associated only with close relatives and were suspicious of strangers in their neighborhoods.

Yet even in Paris, the movement refused to die. By 1943, snipers were shooting at German targets nearly every day. Attacks were so frequent that occupying soldiers did not walk about the city alone and rarely ventured out into the streets at night. Children had to be equally wary in this new atmosphere of hostility. Even in broad daylight, German soldiers often set traps to take their bicycles. It was a dangerous time, yet parents were not overprotective. "What amazes me today," writes Perrault, "is the fact that no one told us to be careful or keep quiet. I suppose it went without saying."[7]

Gradually, as their hunger and misery worsened, and as the oppression of the Nazis grew greater, the people of Paris began to side with the Resistance.

*A celebration for the liberation of Paris at the reclaimed Arc de Triomphe.*

# 6

# PARIS RETURNED

Just a few days after the fall of Paris, French general Charles de Gaulle had broadcast an appeal from London, where he and his small Free French army had fled after the surrender of France. De Gaulle had urged the French to hold on to hope and promised that help would be coming. Few Parisians had taken de Gaulle's message seriously. Germany was far too powerful, its enemies few and weak.

That opinion was confirmed by news reports that came over the radio. The Nazis' lightning assaults continued to overwhelm all opposition, even the huge armies of the Soviet Union. Soviet troops were slammed back hundreds of miles by German troops, who reached the outskirts of Leningrad and Moscow by autumn 1941. It seemed just a matter of time before those cities would fall.

Then on December 7 of that year, Germany's ally, Japan, devastated the United States' Pacific Fleet with a surprise attack on Pearl Harbor. Germany and its allies reigned supreme. Except for the fanatics of the early Resistance movement, few saw any chance that the invincible German army would be driven out of Paris.

Yet, as demoralizing as the Russian offensive and the Pearl Harbor attack were, they signaled the beginning of the end for the conquerors of Paris. The attack on the Soviet Union drained German resources away from western Europe and a possible invasion of England. The Pearl Harbor attack brought the United States off the sidelines and onto the field against Germany and Japan.

For the people of Paris during this time, the radio was their lifeline to hope. No one trusted the information in the local newspapers, which were tightly controlled by the Nazis. New rumors flew around Paris each week, and the tense atmosphere leant credibility to even the most preposterous stories. At one point, the British were said to have developed a new type of chemical that could make water burn. The only sources of information that people could trust were the forbidden broadcasts of the Allied forces. At 9:15 each night, thousands of families crowded around the radio to listen to the war report from the British Broadcasting Corporation (BBC). Many also tuned in to station WRUL, broadcasting out of Boston.

On the night of March 3, 1942, Paris was rocked by terrifying evidence of the power of its friends. Allied bombers struck at a Renault factory that had been producing tanks for the German war effort. Some of the aircraft missed badly in their attack. More than 600 Parisian civilians were killed in the raid, and at least 1,500 were injured. The bombing served notice that, ironically, Paris would suffer far more destruction at the hands of its allies than from the ene-

*Streetlamps in Paris are darkened in case of air attacks.*

my occupying the city.

The air attacks increased as American soldiers and equipment streamed into England. The occupation authorities painted streetlights blue to cut down on the illumination so that Allied bombers would have a more difficult time spotting their targets. The streets were dark, simmering with hostility between the Resistance and the ever-present Gestapo, the threat of a bombing raid always in the air.

Some Parisians bitterly resented the Allied bombs and the destruction they caused. But for the most part, the young people of Paris accepted the hardship as necessary for their liberation. They silently cheered on the Allied pilots, according to Perrault: "We held our breath when a beam [from an air-defense searchlight] picked out a plane. Every bomb that exploded was another blow to loosen the grip of the Nazi oppressors."[1]

As news of German losses in the Soviet Union and North Africa came over the radio in 1943, the people of Paris caught a glimpse of a future without German overlords. They began to hope for a combined American-British invasion from the west. But as weeks went by with no sign of activity, those hopes were cruelly dashed. The failed promise of liberation only made the Parisians' captivity all the harder to bear.

But the Allies were turning the tide of the war. By 1944, waves of Allied planes flew over Paris several times a day. People began to grow used to the air-raid sirens. Instead of panicking at the first sound of a siren, people developed routine procedures to prepare for the attack, which usually arrived 15 minutes after the warning. They took shelter in the metro, closed down their shops, and emptied theaters and other public places. Schoolchildren immediately departed for air-raid shelters. According to Perrault, "the wailing of a siren which interrupted a boring lesson would be greeted with joy."[2] In 1944, children often spent half the school day down in the shelters. Rather than allow the time to go to waste teachers began teaching their lessons in the shelters.

The French suffered yet another blow to their morale when the Allies' wartime strategy again played on their hopes. The British broadcast news of a massive invasion of German-occupied France in the early spring of 1944. The people of Paris believed the stories and leaned on the edges of their chairs each day to hear news of the invasion. Days and then weeks passed, and nothing happened except that food supplies in Paris virtually disappeared. The French were heartbroken. As it turned out, the misleading news had been sent out simply to confuse the Germans so that they would not be prepared for the real attack when it was launched.

The long-awaited assault finally came on Tuesday, June 6, 1944. British, American, and Canadian forces, 176,000 strong, stormed the beaches of Normandy in northwest France. As soon as the BBC broadcast the news, windows flew open on the streets of Paris. A joyful cry of "The English are coming!" echoed across the city.

The Allied forces drove through the German armies in the countryside of France, while Parisians listened to the reports on their radios. There was now no question that Paris would soon be liberated; the German war effort was collapsing on all fronts.

The occupiers, however, were still capable of inflicting enormous cruelty on their captives. The Gestapo exited the scene on a sadistic note, executing 35 young French prisoners whose average age was 17, just days before the liberation armies arrived. Adolf Hitler, furious that his prized French possession would be lost, vowed to destroy the City of Light rather than give it up. He left orders with his commanding officer in the region, Dietrich von

*French sailors and soldiers celebrate the Allied invasion of France and the liberation of their homeland.*

Choltitz, to burn the city to the ground when the Germans abandoned it.

Von Choltitz, however, realized that the order was senseless as well as barbaric. There was no military advantage to be gained by destroying the treasures of Paris. Parisians were spared their greatest agony of the war when the German general ignored Hitler's order.

Meanwhile, the Allied commanders were debating what to do about the still-occupied city. General Dwight Eisenhower, commander of the Allied invasion, saw no reason to waste the resources

of his army on the German garrison in Paris. He knew that the city was in chaos and that restoring order and providing food and services would bog down his army. It made better military sense to bypass the city and keep driving toward Germany to force a surrender as soon as possible.

Rapidly unfolding events in Paris, however, forced him to reconsider. On August 16, the French police finally defied their German governors and went on strike. The next day, General von Choltitz withdrew a large part of the German force, leaving only about 16,000 of his men in the city. After more than four years of humiliation and guilt over their collapse and meek collaboration, the people of Paris were waiting for a chance to redeem themselves. Four to five thousand of them, mainly working-class people, took up whatever arms they could find—old guns, rifles, and knives—and took to the streets.

Few young people had such weapons, but they still managed to get caught up in the wild exhilaration of the moment. Many joined the Resistance and risked enemy fire as they dashed for the weapons of fallen German soldiers. Others helped build barricades in the streets to hinder the movement of the enemy forces. Using turned-over cars, mattresses and furniture hauled out of houses, and paving stones ripped out of the streets, they constructed more than 400 barriers throughout the city. One Parisian marveled at the sight of "young people manning those barricades and laughing at last for the first time in four years."[3]

After four years of cautiously guarding their lives, the people of Paris threw all caution to the wind. Eventually about 50,000 joined in the fight. People leaned out of their windows during the fighting to cheer on their neighbors. Gilles Perrault remembers his father taking him out into the streets to see the fighting. "He knew that this [August 24] would be a day worth living even if it were the last."[4]

The explosion of Paris's pent-up thirst for freedom drove many to daring, reckless acts. Two young Parisians ignored the bullets as they climbed the Eiffel Tower to tear down Germany's swastika and hoist the French tricolor. A 13-year-old boy was shot while hurling a homemade bomb at a German tank.

Yet even in Paris's hour of redemption, the public display of apathy that had shamed so many French clung to the city like a

*Once the liberation of Paris began, the people of Paris united in defending their city.*

*People hit the ground as a sniper opens fire during the fight for the liberation of Paris.*

stain. Entire neighborhoods remained peaceful throughout the three-day fight for liberation. Teenagers were out sunbathing while fighting raged just a few blocks away. So many children were splashing in the Seine River that it looked like a swimming pool.

Persuaded that the liberation of Paris was crucial to the morale of the French people, the Allied commanders agreed to march into the city. On August 25, the Allies arrived, led by the French soldiers of General Jacques Leclerc. By nightfall, the German occupation was over at a cost of perhaps two or three thousand Parisians killed in the final days.

"I have never seen such joy as radiated from the faces of the people of Paris," reported one journalist.[5] Girls climbed on top of tanks and trucks to hug and kiss the liberators, and many of them collected autographs. So many people crowded around the liberating armies that one French soldier said that a tank traveling among them looked like "a magnet passing through a pile of steel filings."[6]

Yet along with the joy came anger. The people burned for revenge on those who had fawned over their German masters, on those who had gotten fat off the misery of others. Young French women who had dated German soldiers were stripped, beaten, and

*Nazi soldiers surrender to victorious French civilians.*

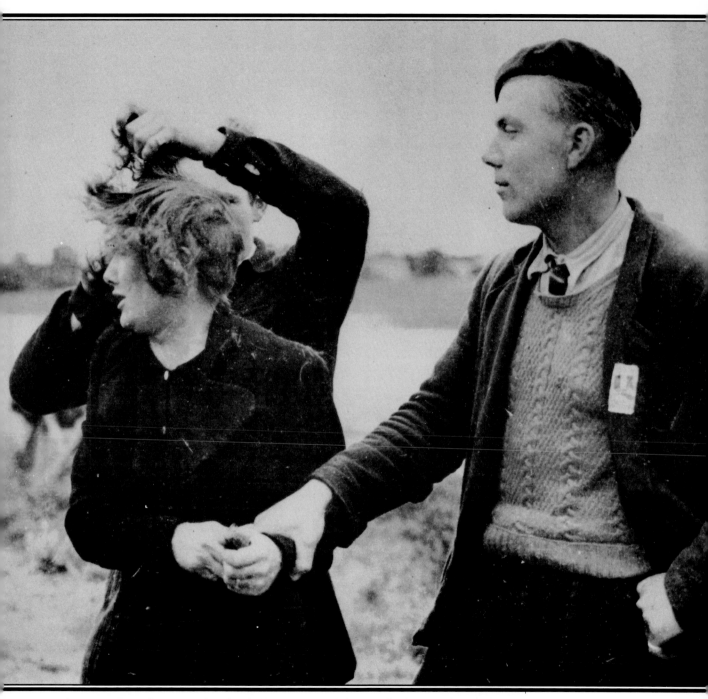

*A young French woman has her hair cut as punishment for her involvement with a German soldier.*

*Trucks filled with supllies enter Paris following the liberation.*

paraded through the streets, their hair shorn, swastikas painted on their foreheads. Collaborators were hunted down. Following liberation, an estimated 100,000 arrests were made in the Paris region alone. More French men and women were killed by the French after the liberation than by the Germans during the occupation.

The scars of the occupation would take a long time to heal; many would remain forever. Hunger had left its mark. One American soldier toured the city with a girl who appeared to be about 12.

*People outside of Paris give the "V for Victory" sign as Allied soldiers make their way to the freed city.*

He later discovered she was 18.

Nor did liberation bring instant relief from the poverty. For many months after the war, food remained hard to find. One visitor wrote that "you don't throw apple cores in the wastebasket. You fling them out the window so that they can be eaten."[7] Automobiles were so scarce that only top government officials, the critically ill, and women about to give birth were allowed to ride in taxis. Rampant inflation destroyed whatever meager earnings the people could eke out. Buildings remained cold in the winter. Strikes and food riots broke out as desperate people searched for a way out of their poverty. Many young people said they would gladly leave France for good if they could.

The city was left with the scars of guilt and a lingering sense of betrayal. Parisians were haunted by the specter of being the only European country in which the people had overwhelmingly supported collaboration with the Nazis. Political parties on the Right and the Left clashed as the young people of France were forced to question themselves and their traditions as the citizens of few nations had ever done.

Yet Paris retained its gift for charm and beauty even in the face of such anguish. Postwar visitors commented that the French were more apt than the people of other war-torn nations to disguise their poverty and take pride in their appearance. Paris recovered its shaken pride to regain its position as the fashion capital of the world, the City of Light, and grew to become the largest metropolitan area in continental Europe.

*A young Parisian boy celebrates the liberation of his city, wearing a hat made out of the French and American flags.*

# SOURCE NOTES

★ ★ ★

**CHAPTER ONE**

1. "Paris in the Spring," *Time* (May 24, 1943), 29.
2. Gilles Perrault and Pierre Azima, *Paris Under the Occupation*, trans. Allison Carter and Maximillian Vos (New York: Vendome Press, 1989), 10.
3. Ernest Reymond, *Paris: City of Enchantment* (New York: Macmillan, 1961), 188.
4. Phillippe Boegner, "L'Eté 40," *Le Figaro* (July 21, 1990), 60.
5. Ibid.
6. Frank to Aaseng, July 30, 1991.
7. Boegner, 60.
8. Milton Dank, *The French vs. the French* (Philadelphia: Lippincott, 1974), 61.
9. David Pryce-Jones, *Paris in the Third Reich* (New York: Holt, Rinehart and Winston, 1981), 3.

**CHAPTER TWO**

1. Dank, 45.
2. Boegner, 86.
3. Pryce-Jones, 22.
4. Ibid., 23.
5. Ibid., 157.
6. Perrault and Azima, 13.
7. Boegner, 86.

**CHAPTER THREE**

1. Pryce-Jones, 134.
2. Perrault and Azima, 16.
3. Pryce-Jones, 230.
4. Ibid., 143.
5. Ibid., 105.

**CHAPTER FOUR**

1. Perrault and Azima, 14.
2. Martin Blumenson, *Liberation* (Alexandria, Va.: Time-Life Books, 1978), 122.
3. Pryce-Jones, 98.
4. Frank to Aaseng, July 30, 1991.
5. Blumenson, 118.
6. Pryce-Jones, 95.
7. Perrault and Azima, 27.
8. "Paris in the Spring," 26.
9. Perrault and Azima, 18.

**CHAPTER FIVE**

1. Blumenson, 13.
2. Pryce-Jones, 104.
3. Boegner, 86.
4. Ibid., 84.
5. Dank, 77.
6. Perrault and Azima, 24.
7. Ibid., 22.

**CHAPTER SIX**

1. Perrault and Azima, 16.
2. Ibid., 33.
3. Dank, 218.
4. Perrault and Azima, 55.
5. Blumenson, 141.
6. Ibid., 143.
7. Douglas Botting, *The Aftermath: Europe* (Alexandria, Va.: Time-Life Books, 1983), 10.

# FURTHER READING

★ ★ ★

Blumenson, Martin. *Liberation*. Alexandria, Va.: Time-Life Books, 1978.

Boegner, Phillippe. "L'Eté 40," *Le Figaro*, July 21, 1990.

Botting, Douglas. *The Aftermath: Europe*. Alexandria, Va.: Time-Life Books, 1983.

Collins, Larry, and Dominique LaPierre. *Is Paris Burning?* New York: Simon & Schuster, 1965.

Dank, Milton. *The French vs. the French*. Philadelphia: Lippincott, 1974.

Lottman, Herbert R. *The Purge: The Purification of French Collaborators After World War II*. New York: William Morrow, 1986.

Perrault, Gilles, and Pierre Azima. *Paris Under the Occupation*. Trans. Allison Carter and Maximillian Vos. New York: Vendome Press, 1989.

Pryce-Jones, David. *Paris in the Third Reich*. New York: Holt, Rinehart and Winston, 1981.

Reymond, Ernest. *Paris: City of Enchantment*. New York: Macmillan, 1961.

Worth, Alexander. *France: 1940-1955*. New York: Henry Holt, 1956.

# INDEX

✶ ✶ ✶